Economics

by Shyam Mehta

How to calculate your real income

What to do if you have a deficit

Why you should act now

The Loving Heart Centre, www.lovingheartcentre.net

Shyam Mehta, 1952 –

Economics

Volume 42 of The Loving Heart Centre Collection

ISBN: 978-1-4092-9137-4

My Works

Much of what I have written comes directly from God.

I have written the following more than 50 books:

A Book of Jokes, ISBN: 978-1-4092-9071-1

A Book of Poems, ISBN: 978-1-4092-8831-2

A Man's Guide to Developing Love and Happiness, ISBN: 1-4121-5210-0

A Storybook for Children Asset and Liability Management Tools: A Handbook for Best Practice

Astrology and Dream Analysis, ISBN: 978-1-4092-9024-7

Autobiography of me, ISBN: 978-1-4092-8654-7

Christianity, ISBN: 978-1-4092-9112-1

Economics, ISBN: 978-1-4092-9137-4

Final Thoughts, ISBN: 978-1-4092-8953-1

Future World, ISBN: 978-1-4092-9058-2

God, ISBN: 978-1-4092-8918-0

Health, ISBN: 978-1-4092-9052-0

How to Bring Up a Child: ISBN: 978-1-4092-9718-5

How to Teach Your Child English, ISBN: 978-1-4092-9135-0

How to Teach Your Child General Knowledge, ISBN: 978-1-4092-9104-6

How to Teach Your Child Maths, ISBN: 978-1-4092-9103-9

Human Being Self Analysis Kit, ISBN: 1-4121-5380-8

Indian Marriage, ISBN: 1-4121-5321-2

Indian Philosophy and Religion, ISBN: 1-4121-5211-9

Lessons from Animals, ISBN: 978-1-4092-8897-8

Life Assurance Sector Review(1987)

More Poems and Songs, ISBN: 978-1-4092-9311-8

MUSIC TO BRING YOU CLOSER TO GOD, ISBN: 978-1-4092-9277-7

Natural Medicine

Oxford University, ISBN: 978-1-4092-9098-8

People with no Clothes, ISBN: 1-4121-5365-4

Perfecting Your Emotional Energy Sphere, ISBN: 1-4121-5164-3

Perfecting Your Love Energy Sphere, ISBN: 1-4121-5169-4

Perfecting Your Mental Energy Sphere, ISBN: 1-4121-5165-1

Perfecting Your Physical Energy Sphere, ISBN: 1-4121-5167-8

Perfecting Your Sexual Energy Sphere, ISBN: 1-4121-5163-5

Physics, ISBN: 978-1-4092-9114-5

Poems and Songs, ISBN: 978-1-4092-8885-5

Science, ISBN: 1-4121-5235-6

Shrimad Bhagavad Gita and Commentary, ISBN: 978-1-4092-8758-2

Silva Mehta Cookbook

Spiritual and Religious Journey, ISBN: 1-4121-5206-2

Stories for Children, ISBN: 978-1-4092-8990-6

Swine Flu and Other Matters

The 108 Heads of Lord Patanjali, ISBN: 1-4121-5160-0

The Eight Sacred Texts of India, ISBN: 1-4121-5162-7

The History of the World, ISBN: 1-4121-5166-X

The Psychology of the Mind, ISBN: 978-4092-9042-1

Western Philosophy, ISBN: 1-4121-5207-0

What Men Should Know about Christian Women, ISBN: 1-4121-5450-2

What to do about Swine Flu and Other Matters, ISBN: 978-1-4092-9077-3

Women laid bare, ISBN: 978-1-4092-8960-9

WORKS OF ART TO CURE YOUR EMOTIONAL DIFFICULTIES, ISBN: 978-1-4092-9264-7

Yoga, ISBN: 1-4121-5161-9

Yoga Philosophy and Practice

Yoga: The Iyengar Way by Silva Mehta (Author); Mira Mehta (Joint Author); Shyam Mehta (Joint Author), ISBN-10: 0679722874

Yoga: The Iyengar Way, Part II, ISBN: 978-1-4092-9089-6

Your Self and Mind, ISBN: 1-4121-5208-9

Many of the English language versions of the books can be obtained from most booksellers across the world (some are now out of print). The books are also available or becoming available in Arabic, Bengali, Chinese Mandarin, French, German, Gujarati, Hindi, Italian, Portuguese, Russian, Spanish and Tamil. For the Indian market, some of my books can be bought more cheaply from www.pothi.com.

Preface

There are likely to be significant changes in the world in the next year or two.

Now is the time to start to think about your long term economic interests, particularly if you are one of the many who is not well off.

But this book provides practical tips for both less well off and more well off people.

Shyam Mehta
The Loving Heart Centre
www.lovingheartcentre.net
6 January 2017

The Loving Heart Centre, www.lovingheartcentre.net

Contents

The Loving Heart Centre, www.lovingheartcentre.net

Chapter 1: Government

It has always been a bit of a myth about government. There is never ever any need to aggregate economic quantities and say this is UK GDP, for example.

You live in your world. There are some robbers out there who have significant power. They take your money and sometimes give you a handout. Your income is what you get from selling your time and effort and belongings less the amount the robbers take from you and plus what they give to you.

Why aggregate 5 people's income or 7 million people's or 60 million incomes? It is a useless activity.

Yours is all you need to know about.

Chapter 2: Rent

Often you do not own your own home.

Then you need to pay rent to survive.

The amount you need to pay for a single (double, if you are married) room in your area is an important figure. Let us call it room rent.

It should include shared toilet and kitchen facilities. For example in Criclewood, London where I live a double room (11 sq. m.) is about £650 per month and a single room (7 sq. m.) is about £500 per month.

This is the base figure for economics in your area.

All other services should be expressed as a proportion of this figure of room rent. It turns out that these other costs when expressed in this way do not vary much across the world.

The figure should include all costs of accommodation: heating, lighting, water supply, rates and taxes, insurance, agents' fees and so forth.

These figures are important because it gives you a good idea about what your minimum living costs are.

In some 'posh' areas, there is no single room accommodation for rent. This means that you should if necessary live in a cheaper area.

The Loving Heart Centre, www.lovingheartcentre.net

Chapter 3: Other costs

Let us start with food. In England 2.75 litres of yoghurt or milk per day will cost you about 5 pounds per day. This is your base line food cost.

Other survival costs are very small. You need dental floss, may be 3 pence per day. You may need clothes and shoes, maybe 10 pence per day.

On average there are 30.44 days in a month and so total costs excluding rent average out at £156 per month.

Total costs are therefore about 130% of (single) room rent for a single person.

For a married couple the total cost is 150% of room rent and for a couple with one child it works out at 145% (for one double and one single room), 150% for a couple with two children (two double rooms).

The Loving Heart Centre, www.lovingheartcentre.net

Chapter 4: Property Ownership

If you own your own property, it is best still to think of yourself renting out but from yourself. This is because in times when you are in need you could always rent out your spare rooms, or rent out your property and find a room somewhere else to live in.

So, add the room rent for the number of rooms that you own (i.e. in total how much you could rent your property out for) to your income and also have the relevant proportion (e.g. if you are one or two people, only one room) of that figure included in your outgo.

The Loving Heart Centre, www.lovingheartcentre.net

Chapter 5: Other Assets

With your investments and so forth, it is best for you to divide the value by (2039- year) and treat this as income. For example, if you are reading this book in 2017, then you divide your non property assets valuation by 22. For example, if you are Bill Gates, then your real non property) income is 10000000000000/22.

The year 2039 is the year when money ceases to count and Western civilization will have succeeded in destroying not just the marital institution, the environment, the food supply but money aswell.

The Loving Heart Centre, www.lovingheartcentre.net

Chapter 6: Net Income

So, now you can calculate your surplus (or deficit) income:

- The income categories could be for example:
- Net income from your job (but, when will you retire?)
- Net income from renting your property, typically 4% pa of the value of your property)
- Income equivalent of investments owned (see above)
- Royalties, misc income
- Pension (your employer may be able to give you an idea how much this will be when you retire)
- State pension (you can look online for this figure in the UK at least, it depends mainly on how many years you paid National Insurance Contributions for)
- Social security scrounge money

You are then able to calculate net income, that is total income from the list above minus the costs of 150% or whatever of room rent discussed previously, based on the number of people who rely on you for your income.

You either have a deficit or a surplus. If you have a surplus and it looks like this will continue into the future, nothing more needs be done. Further economics is an academic exercise. Keep whatever spare cash you may need for a rainy day in the bank or if you live in a secure area under the mattress, or if you are Bill Gates in gold coins in a Swiss Bank vault. My article on my website www.lovingheartcentre.net: 'Investing on the Stock Market and in Property'.

You really need to do two calculations, one for now and one for when you have retired.

Chapter 7: If You Have a Deficit

Well you can do several things:

- Move to a cheaper area
- Sell your house
- Look for a mate to support you
- Maybe see if there is additional income you could make
- Get rid of some of your young dependents. Traditionally, at age 9 people started work and got married, and even before that age they helped their parents in the house or in the fields.

Chapter 8: Moving to a Cheaper Area

The best is to think whether it is practical to do that soon.

Moving house or room is going to become less and less easy over the next ten or so years. Crime, disease etc will become prevalent, see my book 'Future World'.

When on the move your property could well be stolen.

You may well be in pain and not wishing to move.

Chapter 9: Selling Your Home

If you have a deficit, the best bet is to sell your home now.

Selling a property will become a big challenge in the future even though in my view property prices will not radically fall. Property prices will not fall because even though money will cease to have value from 2039, people will not believe it until it is too late. Natural disasters will hit and destroy much available housing stock, pushing up the demand for the remaining stock (see my website article, 'Coping with the forthcoming world natural disasters').

Selling now is advantageous because the cash you get is more than the rent you pay for the remaining 22 years when money will have value.

However, it is advantageous to buy or keep a property if you do not have regular income, rather than keep money in a bank which may fail at any time.

Chapter 10: Security of Bank Assets

It is in my opinion it is likely that in most countries many banks will fail, see my website article 'Bank and Government Default Prospects' which anlyzes the position for a relatively safe bank like HSBC.

.

If you are poor that does not matter, and if you are rich that does not matter either because your assets are spare.

Identity theft is not going to grow as a big issue because people will be more concerned about managing with pain.

But, theft of possessions will be much more commonplace and so you need to have your wits about you and to be fleet of foot. You will need to keep important documentation with you, on person.

Chapter 11: State Pensions

In my opinion, in most countries around the world, these will continue to be paid at around current levels, until 1939.

Chapter 12: Hungry Dogs

When a dog gets hungry it will do anything for food. Well in my view it will be people rather than dogs that you will most need to be afraid of in the long term.

The domestic dogs will have died off through lack of food – see my book "What to do about Swine Flu and Other Matters".

Chapter 13: Future World

In my view the world will look as outlined in my book "Future World", very different from now in most regards, and with huge issues that will not be pleasant.

Conclusion

There are things that you should do now to ensure as best you can a reasonable future for yourself. For example, to sell your house if you have a deficit.

If you have a deficit likely in the future, to move now to a cheaper area to live in, and to downsize: live in one room rather than a mansion.

Economics is simple. There are thousands of books, each hundreds of pages long 'explaining' economics. They are rubbish. One economist thinks this and another thinks that. They do not focus on the essentials, which is what this book does.

So, to sum up, you need to calculate your income and then subtract your necessary outgo. If you have a surplus all well and good. If you have a deficit you need to try and do something about it. Simple is it not?

In this book I show exactly how you can calculate your real income, and also your necessary outgo.

I also set out ways you can adjust if you have a deficit.

Of course a few of you will know that you have a surplus and then you do not need to read this book. But most people are close to the borderline and then this book is very useful.

www.ingramcontent.com/pod-product-compliance
Lightning Source LLC
Chambersburg PA
CBHW021851170526
45157CB00006B/2394